Christmas

By ALLAN MOREY

Illustrations by STEPH HINTON

Music by MARK OBLINGER

CANTATA
LEARNING

WWW.CANTATALEARNING.COM

CANTATA
LEARNING

Published by Cantata Learning
1710 Roe Crest Drive
North Mankato, MN 56003
www.cantatalearning.com

Library of Congress Control Number: 2017007557
978-1-68410-013-2 (hardcover/CD)

Christmas by Allan Morey
Illustrated by Steph Hinton
Music by Mark Oblinger

Book design, Tim Palin Creative
Editorial direction, Flat Sole Studio
Executive musical production and direction, Elizabeth Draper
Music arranged and produced by Mark Oblinger

Printed in the United States of America in North Mankato, Minnesota.
072017   0367CGF17

ACCESS THE MUSIC!

SCAN
CODE
WITH
MOBILE
APP

CANTATALEARNING.COM

TIPS TO SUPPORT LITERACY AT HOME

WHY READING AND SINGING WITH YOUR CHILD IS SO IMPORTANT

Daily reading with your child leads to increased academic achievement. Music and songs, specifically rhyming songs, are a fun and easy way to build early literacy and language development. Music skills correlate significantly with both phonological awareness and reading development. Singing helps build vocabulary and speech development. And reading and appreciating music together is a wonderful way to strengthen your relationship.

READ AND SING EVERY DAY!

TIPS FOR USING CANTATA LEARNING BOOKS AND SONGS DURING YOUR DAILY STORY TIME

1. As you sing and read, point out the different words on the page that rhyme. Suggest other words that rhyme.

2. Memorize simple rhymes such as Itsy Bitsy Spider and sing them together. This encourages comprehension skills and early literacy skills.

3. Use the questions in the back of each book to guide your singing and storytelling.

4. Read the included sheet music with your child while you listen to the song. How do the music notes correlate to the words of the song?

5. Sing along on the go and at home. Access music by scanning the QR code on each Cantata book. You can also stream or download the music for free to your computer, smartphone, or mobile device.

Devoting time to daily reading shows that you are available for your child. Together, you are building language, literacy, and listening skills.

Have fun reading and singing!

Christmas is December 25. It is of one the most celebrated holidays in the world. People sing Christmas carols and give each other presents. Many people enjoy the tradition of having a Christmas tree and decorating their homes. Christmas is a festive time to celebrate with family and have big holiday feasts.

To learn why Christmas is such a merry holiday, turn the page and sing along!

It's a merry time of year!

It's a joyful time of year. (Joyful, joyful)
It's **Christmastime**. Let's cheer
for **ornaments** and lights
blinking brightly in the night.

It's a joyful time of year. (Joyful, joyful!)
It's Christmastime. Let's cheer
for Santa and his toys.
He's bringing gifts for girls and boys.

It's a joyful time of year. (Joyful, joyful!)
It's Christmastime. Let's cheer
for gifts under the tree—
some for you and some for me.

It's a joyful time of year. (Joyful, joyful!)
It's Christmastime. Let's cheer
for **carolers** singing.
Hear the sleigh bells jing-a-ling.

It's a merry time of year!

It's a joyful time of year. (Joyful, joyful!)
It's Christmastime. Let's cheer
for big holiday feasts,
candy canes, and other treats.

It's a joyful time of year. (Joyful, joyful!)
It's Christmastime. Let's cheer
for sledding down a hill—
wheeeeee, oh, what a thrill!

16

It's a joyful time of year.
(Joyful, joyful!)
It's Christmastime. Let's cheer
for icicles and snow
and mugs of hot cocoa.

19

It's a joyful time of year. (Joyful, joyful!)
It's Christmastime. Let's cheer
for **reindeer** and **elves**
and everything else.

It's a merry time of year!

SONG LYRICS
Christmas

It's a merry time of year!
It's a joyful time of year. (Joyful, joyful!)
It's Christmastime. Let's cheer
for ornaments and lights
blinking brightly in the night.

It's a joyful time of year. (Joyful, joyful!)
It's Christmastime. Let's cheer
for Santa and his toys.
He's bringing gifts for girls and boys.

It's a joyful time of year. (Joyful, joyful!)
It's Christmastime. Let's cheer
for gifts under the tree—
some for you and some for me.

It's a joyful time of year. (Joyful, joyful!)
It's Christmastime. Let's cheer
for carolers singing.
Hear the sleigh bells jing-a-ling.

It's a merry time of year!
It's a joyful time of year. (Joyful, joyful!)
It's Christmastime. Let's cheer
for big holiday feasts,
candy canes, and other treats.

It's a joyful time of year. (Joyful, joyful!)
It's Christmastime. Let's cheer
for sledding down a hill—
wheeeeeee, oh, what a thrill!

It's a joyful time of year. (Joyful, Joyful)
It's Christmastime. Let's cheer
for icicles and snow
and mugs of hot cocoa.

It's a joyful time of year. (Joyful, joyful!)
It's Christmastime. Let's cheer
for reindeer and elves
and everything else.
It's a merry time of year!

Christmas

Motown
Mark Oblinger

Intro

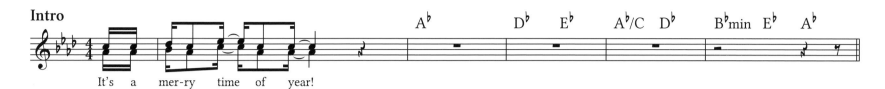

It's a mer-ry time of year!

Verse

1. It's a joy - ful time of year. (Joy - ful, joy - ful!) It's Christ-mas - time. Let's cheer for or - na - ments and lights blink-ing

bright-ly in the night. It's a mer-ry time of year!

Verse 2
It's a joyful time of year. (Joyful, joyful!)
It's Christmastime. Let's cheer
for Santa and his toys.
He's bringing gifts for girls and boys.

Verse 3
It's a joyful time of year. (Joyful, joyful!)
It's Christmastime. Let's cheer
for gifts under the tree—
some for you and some for me.

Verse 4
It's a joyful time of year. (Joyful, joyful!)
It's Christmastime. Let's cheer
for carolers singing.
Hear the sleigh bells jing-a-ling.
It's a merry time of year!

Verse 5
It's a joyful time of year. (Joyful, joyful!)
It's Christmastime. Let's cheer
for big holiday feasts,
candy canes, and other treats.

Verse 6
It's a joyful time of year. (Joyful, joyful!)
It's Christmastime. Let's cheer
for sledding down a hill—
wheeeeee, oh, what a thrill!

Verse 7
It's a joyful time of year. (Joyful, joyful!)
It's Christmastime. Let's cheer
for icicles and snow
and mugs of hot cocoa.

Verse 8
It's a joyful time of year. (Joyful, joyful!)
It's Christmastime. Let's cheer
for reindeer and elves
and everything else.
It's a merry time of year!

23

GLOSSARY

Christmastime—the Christmas season

carolers—people who sing Christmas songs

elves—small imaginary creatures who have magical powers

ornaments—items used for decoration

reindeer—deer native to the far north

GUIDED READING ACTIVITIES

1. Christmas is a time for decorations. Draw a tree, and then decorate it with blinking lights and colorful ornaments.

2. Christmas is a winter holiday. What other holidays do people celebrate during the winter?

3. People celebrate Christmas by decorating their homes and giving presents. Can you think of any other holidays that people celebrate by putting up decorations and giving gifts? How do they decorate their homes? What do they give each other?

TO LEARN MORE

Felix, Rebecca. *We Celebrate Christmas in Winter.* Ann Arbor, MI: Cherry Lake, 2015.

Keogh, Josie. *Christmas.* New York: PowerKids Press, 2013.

Landau, Elaine. *What Is Christmas?* Berkeley Heights, NJ: Enslow, 2012.

Owen, Ruth. *Christmas Sweets and Treats.* New York: Windmill Books, 2013.